the
anger workbook
for teens

activities to help
you deal with **anger**
and **frustration**

RAYCHELLE CASSADA LOHMANN, MS

Instant Help Books
An Imprint of New Harbinger Publications, Inc.

Publisher's Note

Distributed in Canada by Raincoast Books

Copyright © 2009 by Raychelle Cassada Lohmann
        Instant Help Books
        An imprint of of New Harbinger Publications, Inc.
        5674 Shattuck Avenue
        Oakland, CA 94609
        www.newharbinger.com

Cover design by Amy Shoup

Library of Congress Cataloging-in-Publication Data

Lohmann, Raychelle Cassada.
 The anger workbook for teens : activities to help you deal with anger and frustration / Raychelle Cassada Lohmann ; foreword by Julia V. Taylor.
    p. cm.
  ISBN-13: 978-1-57224-699-7 (pbk.)
  ISBN-10: 1-57224-699-5 (pbk.)
  ISBN-13: 978-1-57224-820-5 (pdf ebook)
  ISBN-10: 1-57224-820-3 (pdf ebook)
  1. Anger in adolescence--Juvenile literature. I. Title.
  BF724.3.A55L64 2009
  155.5'1247--dc22
  2009038437

19   18   17

25 24 23 22 21 20 19 18 17 16

contents

✳ contents

foreword

I am honored to write the foreword to Raychelle's book. I have had the distinct pleasure of working with Raychelle and seeing her precise, forward-thinking counseling skills in action. As a high school counselor, we constantly deal with a spectrum of anger issues. Raychelle is always cool, calm, and collected—vital character traits one must possess when defusing angry teenagers.

Anger is a normal and sometimes necessary emotion. It is when it interferes with school, family, and social life that it's a problem. Raychelle approached me years ago with the idea for this workbook. She had been implementing her tools and techniques throughout the school year, noting the ones that were effective, and tossing the ones that weren't. Each activity in *The Anger Workbook for Teens* is a tried and true method— they simply work.

The Anger Workbook for Teens is a phenomenal tool to help teenagers explore, gain knowledge, and ultimately control their emotions. Learning the root of the problem is essential in alleviating it. It will teach readers where their anger stems from and instantly recognize situations that provoke them. In addition, the activities are not time consuming, cheesy, or overly methodical.

Truth be told, I received a copy of the manuscript to write this foreword in April of 2009, six weeks before my school year was ending. I had a student who was constantly sent out of class for his anger outbursts and had tried everything I could think of to help him. Frustrated myself, I opened the copy I had of Raychelle's manuscript and found a few activities. We worked on his "Family Tree" and recognized that his father reacts the same way he does. Next, we talked about the stages of anger and quickly realized that his button pusher was when he thought teachers were embarrassing or dismissive. We worked on different ways to ask questions in class and control his emotions. By then he seemed willing and able to explore his part in the constant referrals. He realized that his body language and smart-alecky outbursts played a large role in irritating his teachers and worked through more appropriate ways to get his questions answered and needs met. He didn't get sent out for the rest of the year and thanked me for "helping me not get so mad and stuff." A highly regarded compliment from the toughest of critics!

Whether you are a teenager, teacher, parent, or counselor, you will find this workbook helpful. It is by far the best anger workbook for teens that I have *ever* come across. I am thankful to have such a useful tool! How awesome it is to be willing to gain control over your anger as a teenager? Kudos to all of the teens willing to go out of their comfort zones and combat it!

Julia V. Taylor

Dear Reader,

Do you often find yourself in trouble because of anger? Do you react to situations and later regret how you behaved? Does your anger cause problems with other people? Are you tired of letting anger control you? If you answered yes to any of these questions, *The Anger Workbook for Teens* is for you.

First and foremost, it is important to understand that anger is a natural human emotion, but people handle it differently. Some hold in their anger and let it build, some lash out with hurtful words, some resort to fighting, and some just explode. No matter how you handle it, you are reading this book because you or someone who cares about you thinks you have a problem with anger.

You are not alone. Anger affects millions of teens, who often find themselves lonely and depressed. They may feel like their relationships are less meaningful or as though they just don't care anymore.

The activities in this workbook will help you notice things that make you angry, handle frustrating situations without getting angry, and effectively communicate your feelings. Most of all, these activities can help you learn to change how you respond to anger. Change is not easy, but with the right frame of mind and set of skills, you can do it. So let's get started!

Wishing you success,

Raychelle Cassada Lohmann

Terrence was having a really bad day. Mr. Williams, Terrence's English teacher, noticed that he seemed angry about something. "Oh no," thought Mr. Williams, "Terrence is in one of his moods. He's so smart and talented, but his anger is really hurting him. He's going to get into trouble if he doesn't turn it around."

After class, Mr. Williams called Terrence over and said, "You take everything so seriously, Terrence. Your anger is beginning to get in the way of your schoolwork, and I'm really worried about you. You've been suspended three times this year and you're constantly in the principal's office. Let me help you. What do you say?"

Terrence knew that Mr. Williams was right. So he nodded his head and said, "Yeah, okay...."

"Great," Mr. Williams said. "We'll begin by taking a good look at your anger. Once we see what effect it has on you, we can start to come up with a plan to help you manage it."

for you to do

This activity will help you gauge how much of a problem your anger is and begin to understand how it affects your life.

Read each statement and check either "Yes" or "No."

People have often commented on my anger.	☐ Yes	☐ No
My anger gets me into trouble.	☐ Yes	☐ No
I have occasionally become so angry that later I could not remember what I did.	☐ Yes	☐ No
Other members of my family have anger problems.	☐ Yes	☐ No
I have hit or harmed someone else when I was angry.	☐ Yes	☐ No
I often feel that I am the victim.	☐ Yes	☐ No
I often feel that no one understands me.	☐ Yes	☐ No

For each of these statements, circle the number that best describes you.

I have trouble controlling my anger.

1	2	3	4	5
strongly disagree	disagree	neutral	agree	strongly agree

On average, I get really angry …

1	2	3	4	5
once a month	every two weeks	once a week	every few days	every day

When I get angry, I am most likely to …

1	2	3	4	5
run away from the situation	cry	scream	hit something	destroy something

The more frequently you checked "Yes" and the higher you rated yourself on these scales, the more anger is driving your life. By committing to doing the activities in this book, you will learn skills that will help you get a grip on your anger.

... and more to do!

Has your anger ever hurt you emotionally or physically? Tell how.

_____

_____

_____

_____

_____

Do you ever blame others for your anger? Tell how (for example, by making accusations or denying that you did something).

_____

_____

_____

When you are angry, do you frequently say or do things that you later regret? Describe a time when this happened.

_____

_____

_____

What do you do to calm down when you're angry? Does it work?

_____

_____

_____

If you could change one thing about yourself, what would it be?

_____

_____

_____

_____

_____

making a game plan 2

for you to know

Making a game plan is a great way to tackle changing things about yourself that are causing you problems. When you make something a priority, you'll be more motivated to get it done. And, the more motivated you are, the harder you'll work to change.

There are thirty-six more activities in this workbook. If you try to do an activity a day, you may be rushing through the workbook and not getting the full benefit. If you do two or three a week, you will have time to think about what you are learning and apply it to your life.

Give yourself time to do each activity and to practice using some of the skills you are learning before taking on the next one. It's important to do all of the activities in the order they appear. The skills become more complex as you go along, and each activity builds on the ones that precede it.

Here are some important things to remember as you develop your plan:

- Schedule a time to work on your activities and treat the time like an assignment. You'll be more likely to stick to your plan that way.

- Practice the skills you are learning. The more something is part of your everyday life, the more likely you are to change.

- Don't fly through the activities. Go slowly and reflect on what you have learned.

- Focus on what you've already accomplished as opposed to what you still have left to do. The remaining job will then seem more manageable.

for you to do

Write out a schedule for working on the activities. If something comes up and you have to change your plan, that's okay. In fact, you may want to do this activity in pencil so you can go back and make changes.

Anger Workbook Schedule		
Date to Begin	Activity	Date Completed
	3. Setting Goals and Creating Action Plans	
	4. Rewarding Yourself	
	5. Keeping an Anger Log	
	6. Recognizing Your Anger Buttons	
	7. Understanding Family Patterns	
	8. Your Body's Response to Anger	
	9. Fight or Flight	
	10. Masking Your Emotions	
	11. The Media and Anger	
	12. Using Anger for Positive Results	
	13. Chilling Out	
	14. Writing	
	15. Laughing at Anger	
	16. Taking a Mental Vacation	
	17. Releasing Anger Symbolically	
	18. Relaxation Techniques	

Date to Begin	Activity	Date Completed
	19. Handling Anger Constructively	
	20. Anger Contract	
	21. Taking Responsibility for Your Own Actions	
	22. Keeping Perspective	
	23. Getting the Facts	
	24. Stages of Anger	
	25. Perception	
	26. Weighing the Options	
	27. The ABC Model of Anger	
	28. Coping with Conflict	
	29. Using I-Messages	
	30. Good Listening	
	31. Complimenting Others	
	32. Body Language	
	33. Communicating Clearly	
	34. Being Assertive	
	35. Steps Toward Change	
	36. Seeing How Far You Have Come	
	37. Anger Certificate	

... and more to do!

You can increase your chances of sticking to your plan by following these tips:

- Work on the activities at the same time daily, such as right after school.

- Commit to working on the activities for a set amount of time each day, perhaps fifteen minutes.

- Tell a trusted friend that you're working on the activities so that you have someone supporting you as you make progress.

What other ways can you think of to increase your chances of sticking to your plan?

_____

_____

_____

What goals have you had in the past that required you to make a game plan?

_____

_____

_____

Do you think having a plan helped you achieve those goals? Tell why or why not.

_____

_____

_____

Do you have any other goals that might benefit from a plan? If so, what are they?

_____

_____

_____

3 setting goals and creating action plans

for you to know

There are two types of goals: short-term and long-term. Short-term goals are ones you will achieve in the near future, such as within a day or a week. Long-term goals are ones you will achieve in a longer period of time, such as a month or a year. The steps you take to achieve your goals make up your action plan.

Antonio was constantly in trouble. He was failing two courses and he was always fighting with his parents. If he didn't like how other kids looked at him, he was in their faces in a heartbeat: "What are you looking at, punks!" Shoving, pushing, talking back, and slamming things around were his ways of dealing with life.

One day, Antonio realized that it was time for a change. The person he had become on the outside wasn't his real self. He felt like he was in a tug-of-war with his anger—and his anger was winning. He went to see his school counselor, Ms. Lee, who offered to help him.

"The first step," said Ms. Lee, "is to develop some goals. Think of a mountain climber who starts at the foot of a mountain. His long-term goal is to reach the summit before nightfall. He breaks up the climb into smaller segments so that it doesn't seem so overwhelming; those segments are his short-term goals. He also has an action plan, which is his strategy for reaching each goal. You can take the same approach to getting your anger under control."

Working with Ms. Lee, Antonio came up with these goals and actions plans.

Long-Term Goal: I will control my anger.

Action Plan:

1. I will learn to talk about what bothers me rather than getting angry.

2. I will learn to compromise.

3. I will learn to focus on the positive side of situations.

Short-Term Goal: I will fight less often in the next month.

Action Plan:

1. I will not provoke, name-call, push, or hit anyone.

2. I will ask for help when I feel frustrated.

3. I will take ten deep breaths when I find myself wanting to yell at my parents.

With his goals and plan in place, Antonio was on his way to change.

for you to do

Setting goals for yourself is an important step toward change. In the space that follows, write down two anger goals for yourself: one long-term and one short-term. Then add your action plans, which are the steps you will take to reach each goal.

My Anger Goals and Action Plans

Long-Term Goal: _____

_____

Action Plan: _____

_____

_____

Short-Term Goal: _____

_____

Action Plan: _____

_____

_____

... and more to do!

What other areas of your life would benefit from your setting goals and creating an action plan? Some possibilities include school, work, and relationships.

_____

_____

_____

Choose one of these areas, and set a long-term goal and a short-term goal. Then create an action plan for these goals.

Long-Term Goal: _____

_____

Action Plan: _____

_____

_____

_____

Short-Term Goal: _____

_____

Action Plan: _____

_____

_____

_____

4   rewarding yourself

for you to know

It's a good idea to reward yourself when you accomplish one of your anger-management goals. Why? The answer is simple: It makes you feel good! And that's not the only reason. Rewards are motivating, and the more motivation you have to do something, the harder you'll try.

Learning to manage your anger isn't going to be easy, but rewards can help you reach your goals. A reward provides you with motivation to do something that might otherwise be hard for you. For example, if you're trying to stop yelling at your mom, your reward might be that you get to blog on the computer if you make it through dinner without yelling. The goal is not to yell, and the reward is blogging on the computer.

Here are some other rewards you might choose:

- seeing a movie
- downloading new music
- shopping
- going to a concert
- eating out at your favorite restaurant
- hanging out with friends
- skateboarding
- riding your bike
- shooting hoops

for you to do

Next to each treasure chest, write down what you would like to reward yourself with and the date you will try to earn the reward by. When you have reached a goal, write down what you achieved. Try to earn all of your rewards!

I will work to achieve this reward: _____

I plan to earn this reward by this date: _____

To earn this reward, I _____

_____.

I will work to achieve this reward: _____

I plan to earn this reward by this date: _____

To earn this reward, I _____

_____.

I will work to achieve this reward: _____

I plan to earn this reward by this date: _____

To earn this reward, I _____

_____.

I will work to achieve this reward: _____

I plan to earn this reward by this date: _____

To earn this reward, I _____

_____.

... and more to do!

Look back at the goals you set in Activity 3 and share them with a friend or family member whom you trust. Ask this person to notice when you meet one of your goals and to remind you to give yourself a reward. Keep a record of all of the goals you've achieved and rewards you've received. If you become discouraged, you can look back at this activity and see how far you've come!

I Did It!		
Goal I Reached	Reward I Received	Date I Received It

---

for you to know

It is important to become aware of situations that make you angry, to notice what you do when you get angry, and to recognize the consequences of your anger. An anger log is a tool to help you do all that.

Michelle had been waiting all week for Alicia to come over for a sleepover. They had big plans for Saturday night, and Michelle was literally counting down the minutes. Saturday morning around ten, Alicia texted her: "no good 4 2nite. have 2 do it another time." "Are you for real?" Michelle thought.

This wasn't the first time Alicia had stood Michelle up. She felt like she couldn't count on Alicia for anything. The more she thought about it, the angrier she became. Before she knew it, Michelle grabbed a shoe and threw it at the wall—hard. It landed on her desk and knocked over some pictures, which fell and broke. Her parents heard the commotion and ran to her room, only to find a mess. The result? Michelle was grounded for two weeks.

Later that afternoon, when Michelle had calmed down, her mom said to her, "Honey, you seem to get angry at Alicia so often, and the results are never good. It might help if you could see the patterns. That way, you could start to think about more helpful ways to react."

Keeping a log can help you see patterns in your anger. This sample entry shows you how Michelle might have recorded what happened with Alicia.

Anger Log	
Date and Time:	October 3, 10 a.m.
What Happened:	Alicia texted last minute and can't stay over.
What I Was Thinking:	She always makes excuses. I am sick of being her friend.
What I Was Feeling:	Furious, disappointed, and hurt
What I Did:	Threw a shoe at my desk
What My Consequences Were:	Trouble with parents. Broke some of my favorite pictures. Grounded for two weeks.
How I Handled It:	Not well. I am going to be a hermit for the next few weeks. Not to mention I have a mess to clean up.
What I Could Have Done Instead:	Told Alicia that I was angry about her constant excuses, then called another friend to come over or asked my sister if she was up for a movie.

for you to do

Before you start, make several photocopies of this blank log. For as long as you are working on the activities in this book, keep your anger log.

Anger Log	
Date and Time:	
What Happened:	
What I Was Thinking:	
What I Was Feeling:	
What I Did:	
What My Consequences Were:	
How I Handled It:	
What I Could Have Done Instead:	

... and more to do!

Once you've made a few entries in your log, see if you notice a pattern of when you get angry.

Is there any particular time of the day when this occurs (for example, in the evening when you are tired or trying to do homework, or in the morning when you first wake up)?

_____

_____

_____

Do you seem to get angry in certain situations or with particular people?

_____

_____

_____

Are there specific areas you think you can work on?

_____

_____

_____

After a few weeks, review your log. Have you seen an improvement in the way you handle your anger? If so, tell what has changed.

_____

_____

_____

for you to know

We all have buttons that when pushed lead to anger. Some people call these buttons "pet peeves" or "triggers." No matter what you call them, it's important that you identify the things that bug you and head them off before your anger builds.

Tabitha came up to Leigha in the hall and accused her of taking Jessica's textbook from her locker. Leigha hadn't even gone to Jessica's locker! She tried to explain, but Tabitha interrupted and said, "Josh told us he saw you in Jessica's locker this morning, and now her history book is missing. Her homework was inside that book. Just give it back so she doesn't get a bad grade."

Leigha's fists clenched, and she raised her voice. "Tabitha, for the last time, I don't have Jessica's stuff!" But Tabitha would not back down. She got right in Leigha's face and called her a liar. That did it! Being accused of lying always set Leigha off. She threw down her books and knocked Tabitha's stuff out of her hands. "You did not just call me a liar!"

Just like Leigha, we all have things that push our buttons. Here are some examples of things others do that may push your buttons:

- Nag you
- Tell others something you told them in confidence
- Try to boss you around
- Accuse you of something you didn't do
- Invade your space
- Accuse you of saying something you didn't say

- Make repetitive noises
- Borrow something of yours without permission
- Borrow something of yours and ruin it
- Write nasty things about you
- Go through your things

for you to do

In the column headed "Button," write down things that are very likely to set off your anger. In the next column, write down one thing you can do to release that button when you realize it is being pushed. For example, if being nagged is one of your buttons, you may be able to release it by removing yourself from the situation. Finally, rank your buttons from most annoying to least annoying.

Button	Release	Rank

How can knowing what your buttons are help you with anger?

_____

_____

_____

... and more to do!

On a separate sheet of paper, list your button releases and then make several copies of your list. Put them in places that are readily accessible—for example, your wallet, your backpack, and your nightstand. Review the list often so that the next time you find one of your buttons is being pushed, you can head off an anger situation by recalling your release.

7 understanding family patterns

for you to know

You've probably spent a lot of time around your family, especially when you were little, so naturally you've picked up some of your habits and behaviors from them. Exploring how members of your family interact can help you understand your own response to anger.

Gabrielle's dad had given her a list of chores to do before she could go to the mall with her friends. The more she thought about all the things she had to do, the more upset she got. "Clean this, do that," she muttered. "Do it yourself, Dad!"

Her father heard her and yelled, "If I hear one more smart word out of your mouth, you won't go anywhere! Do I make myself clear?"

"Perfectly!" said Gabrielle, rolling her eyes. She stomped off. She picked up her clothes from the floor and tossed them into the laundry room, kicking the door on her way out. Next, she started to unload the dishwasher. She threw the silverware into the drawer and banged pots around as she put them away.

Her father marched into the kitchen and slammed his hand on the counter. "Listen here, young lady, stop banging stuff around!"

Just then Gabrielle's mother walked into the room. "What on earth is going on here? All I hear is screaming and slamming. You two are like peas in a pod. Gabrielle, you get that temper from your dad's side. They all throw temper tantrums when they don't get their way. Both of you, settle down and get away from each other for a while. Gabrielle, you know the rule: no privileges unless you do your chores. If you're not done in an hour, then you can't go to the mall."

"Okay," Gabrielle sighed. She knew that her mom meant what she said.

for you to do

At the bottom of this tree, write your name. Then add the names of your family members. In the space provided, indicate how they handle anger, such as:

- blows up
- throws things
- says mean things
- walks away from the situation
- goes for a jog
- takes some time alone to calm down
- yells
- holds anger inside

On or near the tree, add the names of other family members—aunts, uncles, cousins, or siblings, for example—whom you have been told you are like.

Circle the name of the person you most resemble in your response to anger. In the space provided, indicate how your parents and grandparents handle anger.

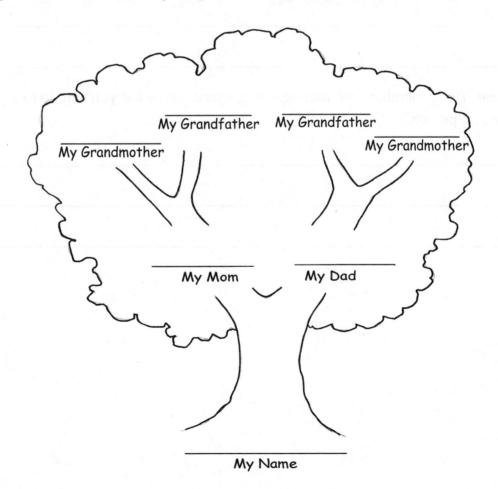

My Grandfather   My Grandfather

My Grandmother   My Grandmother

My Mom   My Dad

My Name

... and more to do!

Did you notice a pattern in how your relatives handle anger? If so, explain.

_____

_____

_____

What was one thing that stood out about how your family members deal with their anger?

_____

_____

_____

Choose one family member who manages anger well. Tell what you can do to try to be more like that person.

_____

_____

_____

your body's response to anger

for you to know

Anger causes stress, which can lead to physical reactions that include high blood pressure, headaches, stomachaches, and heart problems, among others. Not everyone reacts the same way, and learning how anger affects your body will help you recognize when you are becoming angry.

Look at some of the physical ways anger manifests itself. When you get angry, you might experience some of these things:

- cry
- feel your face get hot
- grind your teeth
- roll your eyes
- breathe heavily
- notice that your heart is racing
- break out in a rash
- feel short of breath

- get a headache
- get a stomachache
- sweat
- have nervous twitches
- feel your muscles tighten
- feel dizzy
- feel nauseated

Knowing your physical response to anger can help you become aware of when you need to cool it. These tips can help when you reach that point:

- Take five deep breaths, concentrating on exhaling.

- Excuse yourself from the situation and go for a walk or go to a quiet space.

- If you can't get away from the situation, you can tell yourself to calm down and imagine a relaxing place (perhaps your bedroom, the beach, or your grandmother's house). As you bring this place to mind, focus on letting the anger drain from your body like water from a bathtub.

for you to do

In the outline below, draw in all the parts of your body that are affected when you feel angry. For example, if you cry when you get angry, you might draw eyes with tears. If your muscles get tight, you might draw flexed biceps.

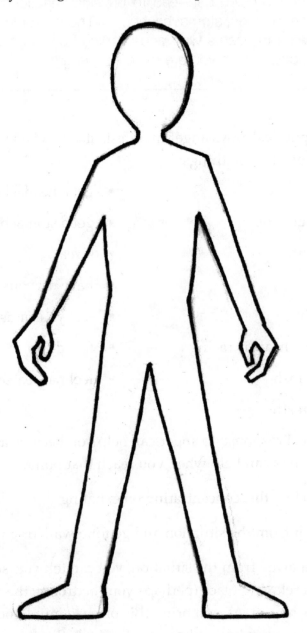

... and more to do!

How does your body respond to anger?

_____

_____

_____

What part of your body is most affected by anger?

_____

_____

_____

In addition to the earlier suggestions, what else can you do to cool down when you feel your body responding to anger?

_____

_____

_____

_____

_____

9　fight or flight

---

for you to know

Each time you sense danger, your body automatically tries to protect you. Adrenaline, a chemical that gives you a quick rush of energy, is released into your bloodstream. Your pupils dilate, your heart rate accelerates, your blood pressure rises, and your breathing speeds up. You become alert and highly sensitive to your surroundings. This combination of reactions is called the fight-or-flight response. How you react to this response can improve situations or make them worse.

Lisa got home from school and went straight to the computer. To her surprise, when she opened Facebook, there was a nasty message from a girl in her math class. "How dare she slam me like that! Who does she think she is?" Lisa thought.

As Lisa continued to read, she wondered, "How many people have seen this? She's ruined my life!" And the more she read, the angrier she became. Her face started to get hot, and her shoulder muscles began to tense. All she could think was: "I'll get her back!"

Lisa was faced with a choice: fight or flight. What do you think she chose? If you guessed fight, you're right. Instead of withdrawing, she reacted by wanting to get back at the other girl.

When you feel your body going into this mode, you can react positively or negatively. Positive reactions can improve the situation, while negative ones only make things worse.

for you to do

Read this situation; put a "P" next to positive reactions and an "N" next to negative reactions.

William had prepared all week for his in-class presentation. When he got up to speak, he noticed his classmates were whispering. Some kids were looking at him and snickering. He tried to concentrate on his presentation, but his mind went blank. When the teacher prompted him to start, he broke into a cold sweat and stared out across the room. All he could think was: "These kids are ruining it for me!" What is William going to do?

_____ Block the class out mentally and try to pretend that they don't exist.

_____ Stop and ask to speak with the teacher in private.

_____ Run out of the room.

_____ Say something like, "Hey, guys, give me a break."

_____ Yell at the class for messing up his presentation.

_____ Throw his materials across the room while screaming, "I've had it!"

Next, read these situations and come up with your own ideas for positive reactions.

Bianca had tried out for the lead in the school play. She really thought she deserved the part, and today the drama coach was posting the cast list. At lunchtime, Bianca joined the crowd of kids at the bulletin board. She read down the list, and her face turned bright red when she saw that Arielle had gotten the lead. And what was worse, Bianca was going to be in the chorus. She wouldn't even have any lines! Just then, Arielle walked up and several of the kids congratulated her. Bianca felt like stomping off. What could she do?

_____

_____

_____

Molly was always borrowing Kim's iPod. One Friday afternoon, Kim asked Molly to return it. "Uh, I don't have it. I let Ian borrow it," Molly replied. Kim couldn't believe her ears. Molly had no right to lend something that didn't even belong to her! Kim was furious with Molly, but she'd deal with that later. First she needed to find Ian and get her iPod back. As Kim approached Ian, she noticed he was holding an iPod—and it looked broken! Her heart started to pound. What could she do?

_____

_____

_____

... and more to do!

Think of a time when your body went into fight-or-flight mode. Describe the situation.

_____

_____

_____

How did your body react?

_____

_____

_____

Tell how you handled the situation and whether you think your response was positive or negative.

_____

_____

_____

Can you think of other positive reactions you might have had?

_____

_____

_____

10 masking your emotions

for you to know

Sometimes it's easier to get mad than to admit that your feelings are hurt or that you're really scared. But masking other emotions with anger is not a positive way to cope with a situation, and it can actually be harmful. Until you deal with your underlying feelings, your anger may continue to grow.

Jake could tell something was up at home. His parents had been arguing constantly. His dad often left and didn't come home until one or two in the morning. His mom cried a lot, and Jake had seen her sitting in the kitchen with a checkbook and calculator, looking worried. Once he overheard them discussing whom he would live with if they separated.

Jake felt anxious about the future and hurt that his parents hadn't told him what was happening. He also felt a bit guilty because he wondered if he was the cause of their arguments.

Finally, one Saturday at breakfast, his parents told him that they would be getting a divorce. Jake immediately felt his stomach knot and his face turn red. He shouted, "That's the worst! I don't even want to talk about it!" He jumped up and stormed away from the table.

His mom called him back. She looked at him closely and said, "Jake, you look so angry, but I know you must have other feelings about this divorce. Let's talk about them." When Jake was able to express the feelings that lay under his anger, he began to feel calmer.

for you to do

This list represents some feelings you may have masked with anger. Circle any that apply to you, and use the blank lines to add others.

hurt	depression	fear
greed	stress	shame
anxiety	frustration	_____
loneliness	jealousy	_____

Tell about a specific time when you masked your feelings with anger.

_____

_____

_____

How would expressing your actual feelings have helped?

_____

_____

_____

... and more to do!

Choose another situation that made you angry and then think about what other emotions might have been at the root of your anger. In the mask below, write down those feelings. If you prefer, you can use the space to create a collage of pictures or words from old magazines or newspapers. When you have finished, look at your mask and think about how you let each of those feelings get replaced by anger.

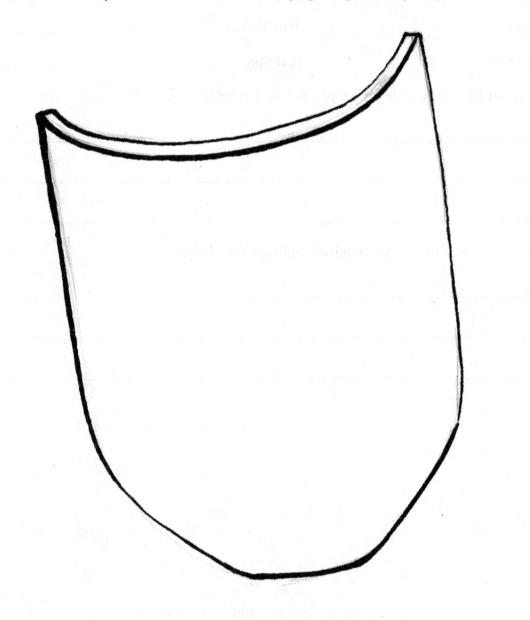

for you to know

The more that people see violence in the media, the more likely they are to act out aggressively. If you reduce your exposure to violent TV shows and video games, you will find it easier to manage your anger.

Did you know that the level of violent behavior in Saturday morning cartoons is higher than in prime-time television? Children's TV shows depict even more violence than shows for adults do, so from the time you were a young child to today, it's likely that you've watched a lot of anger and aggression on TV shows. And TV is not the only source of exposure to violence. Movies, music videos, video games, newspapers, magazines, and the Internet all contribute to the amount of violence you see.

The fast-paced, intense action may get you involved and hold your attention, but it's actually bad for you. Studies have shown that watching lots of violent shows or playing violent games can cause people to react aggressively.

for you to do

For one week, keep a record of how often you are exposed to violence in the media. In the bottom row, add up the incidents of violence. You may be surprised at how much anger and aggression you're seeing!

	Television	Movies	Music Videos	Video Games	Newspapers and Magazines	The Internet
Monday						
Tuesday						
Wednesday						
Thursday						
Friday						
Saturday						
Sunday						
Total						

Which type of media exposed you to the most violence? _____

Adding all columns, how much media violence were you exposed to over the week?

_____

What are your thoughts about the amount of media violence you see?

_____

_____

_____

... and more to do!

Are there certain TV shows or video games you could cut out of your life? Write their titles here.

_____

_____

_____

_____

Make a pledge to reduce the level of media violence you are exposed to. Write it here:

_____

_____

_____

12 using anger for positive results

for you to know

Even though anger has a bad rap, it can be a very useful emotion. Expressing your anger is one way to stand up for your rights and the rights of others. It can help you promote change when you think something is unfair. For example, if Martin Luther King Jr. had not gotten angry, there would be a lot more injustice in this world.

Nathan was on his way home when he saw a boy pushing around a smaller boy. He watched for a minute as the bully kept shoving the other kid. The poor kid didn't have a chance; each time he got up, the bully would shove him again, and he would stumble and fall to the ground.

"That's not right," Nathan thought. "That guy is twice his size. He's going to hurt that kid." He walked toward the bully and called, "Hey, stop! Why don't you leave him alone?"

The bully turned and looked at Nathan. "Why don't you mind your own business?" he responded.

Nathan, who was much taller than the bully, grinned and said, "This is my business."

The bully gave another glance at Nathan. Then he turned back to the kid and said, "You're not worth my time." He headed off.

Nathan went over to the kid. "Are you all right?"

"Yeah," said the kid. "That guy's a real jerk; he pushes everyone around. Thanks for your help."

The next week, Nathan was still really bothered by what had happened, so he met with the principal at his school. He suggested that the students develop a club to teach kids how to stand up against bullies and how to get help from adults. The principal was very excited about Nathan's idea and said, "Nathan, your anger about seeing another student get pushed around will lead to a wonderful program to help others avoid that experience!"

Next time you find yourself getting angry, take your anger and turn it to good. Ask yourself these questions:

- What is within my control?

- How can I be an agent for change?

- What can I do to fix the problem rather than just acting out in anger?

Remember, anger itself is not necessarily a problem. It's how you choose to handle it.

for you to do

Think of a time when you turned your anger into something positive, perhaps by standing up for someone in a difficult situation, or protesting against something you thought was unfair.

Describe the situation.

_____

_____

_____

Tell how you handled the situation.

_____

_____

_____

Are you satisfied with how you reacted? If not, what could you have done differently?

_____

_____

_____

... and more to do!

When people use their anger to stick up for the rights of others, anger is a positive force. These people and organizations changed the world with their anger:

- Dr. Martin Luther King's leadership in the civil rights movement

- Susan B. Anthony's fight for women's right to vote

- Nelson Mandela's fight against apartheid

- MADD (Mothers Against Drunk Driving)

- SAVE (Students Against Violence Everywhere)

Choose one to read about, and tell how anger was channeled into something positive.

_____

_____

_____

_____

_____

_____

_____

_____

_____

13 chilling out

for you to know

When you are angry, choosing an activity that helps you calm down will keep your anger from getting the best of you.

Ethan's younger brother Ryan was a pain in the neck. Whenever Ethan was watching television, Ryan wanted to change the channel. If Ethan was talking on the phone, Ryan would interrupt. He would borrow Ethan's CDs without asking and then forget where he had put them.

One evening at dinner, Ethan was just about to take a slice of watermelon for dessert when Ryan reached across and grabbed the last piece. That was it! Ethan shoved his brother, who started to cry. Their mom sent both boys away from the table.

Later that evening, she knocked on Ethan's door and asked if they could talk. She said, "Ethan, I know that Ryan often bugs you, but shoving him is not acceptable. Let's talk about what you can do to chill out when you feel angry with him." Together, Ethan and his mom came up with this list:

- Talk to someone.
- Take a time-out.
- Text a friend.
- Pound on a pillow.
- Play an instrument.
- Listen to relaxing music.

- Go for a bike ride.
- Play basketball.
- Read a book.
- Draw.
- Write in a journal.

The next time Ethan found himself getting angry with Ryan, he simply stretched out on the sofa with his iPod. Pretty soon, he could hardly remember what had made him so angry!

for you to do

Think about situations that often make you angry. When these situations arise, tell how you can chill out instead of exploding.

I get angry when _____

_____

I can chill out by _____

_____

I get angry when _____

_____

I can chill out by _____

_____

I get angry when _____

_____

I can chill out by _____

_____

... and more to do!

Using old magazines and newspapers, cut out pictures that remind you of your favorite ways to chill out. For example, if swimming helps you chill out, you might add a picture of a swimmer or a lake. Paste the pictures on a blank piece of paper or cardboard. Put your chill-out poster where you are most likely to find it helpful—perhaps in a notebook, on your desk, or in your locker.

writing 14

for you to know

When you hold in your anger, it is likely to build. Expressing your feelings is an important first step toward coping with them, and writing is a great way to do that. How well you write or whether you follow grammar rules is not important in this type of writing. What is important is getting your feelings out.

Exploring your emotions is like dumping out a puzzle and sorting through the pieces. At first, the task may seem overwhelming. But once you begin to match up some pieces, the rest begin to fall into place. Think of writing as a way to help you sort through the puzzle pieces of life.

If you've never expressed your feelings this way before, a great way to start is by writing a letter to yourself. You can pretend that you're writing to a close friend whom you trust with your life. Silly as it may sound, writing a letter to yourself lets you explore your thoughts and feelings. You have no one to impress, so you can be honest about what you want to change about your behavior.

for you to do

Write a letter to yourself. Include things that you are unhappy about, disappointed with, or want to change. Talk about why anger has been a problem for you and why you want to handle it differently.

When you have finished your letter, photocopy it and place the copy in an envelope. Put it somewhere safe and plan to open it in six months. You may be surprised at the changes that you've made!

Dear Me,

Love,

... and more to do!

Journaling is a great way to help you cope with your anger. You can make a habit of writing down your thoughts and feelings rather than bottling them up, especially when something is bothering you. Expressing yourself in writing can help you examine whatever is bugging you. Then you can develop a plan to handle the situation rather than reacting impulsively, which often leads to negative consequences.

15 laughing at anger

---

for you to know

Humor is a great way to defuse anger. Not only can it improve a tense situation, but it's also good for your health! A good laugh reduces your level of stress hormones and boosts your level of endorphins, which are hormones that give you a sense of well-being.

Anger and humor are polar opposites, so it's hard to be angry and laugh at the same time. Look at some of the ways that laughter and anger can affect you.

Laughter:	Anger:
makes you forget about your anger	makes you focus on what you're mad about
makes you feel happy	makes you unhappy
gives you a great stomach workout	causes your heart to beat faster
makes others want to be with you	hurts your relationships with others
decreases tension	makes you tense

A situation that makes you angry is likely to have a different outcome depending on whether you allow your anger to escalate or your sense of humor to take over. Many episodes of anger are actually funny, if you can step away from what has happened long enough to notice. So next time you get angry, stop and ask yourself, "What's funny about this situation?" Chances are you'll find some humor if you just look for it.

for you to do

Jake's dad had reminded him twice to take out the garbage. Jake knew he had to do it, but he was in the middle of a video game and didn't want to be interrupted. At his dad's third reminder, Jake stormed into the kitchen and grabbed the lid off the trash can. He jerked the garbage bag out with so much force that it burst open and trash flew across the kitchen floor. To make things even worse, Jake slipped on the remains of that evening's dinner! When his father came into the kitchen to see what all the commotion was about, he found Jake lying on the floor surrounded by trash.

Write an ending that shows what might have happened if Jake continued to allow his anger to take over.

_____

_____

_____

_____

Next, write an ending that shows Jake finding some humor in what happened.

_____

_____

_____

_____

... and more to do!

Think of a time when you reacted to a situation with anger. Describe the situation and what you did.

_____

_____

_____

_____

_____

_____

Imagine you had been able to find humor in this situation, and rewrite your experience showing how the outcome would have been different.

_____

_____

_____

_____

_____

_____

for you to know

Having a special place where you feel comfortable and relaxed can help when you're upset. Even if you can't actually visit it, just going there in your imagination can help you clear your head and calm yourself.

Kayla was having a terrible day. All of her friends had turned against her at school because of a rumor that wasn't even true. She thought, "Whoever started that rumor is going to regret ever mentioning my name!" She couldn't wait until she got home. She just wanted to go to her room and close out the world.

TJ's girlfriend had just broken up with him over the weekend, and she was already going out with another guy. He was furious with her and upset that everyone would realize she had dumped him. If he could only disappear for a while … maybe go to the beach where his problems would seem so small compared to the ocean. He had a lot of good memories of times at the beach and always felt relaxed when he was there.

Have you ever felt like Kayla or TJ? Do you have a place you like to escape to when things aren't going well? You may not always be able to go to that special place right away. That's okay; you can still take a mental vacation and just imagine being there.

for you to do

Imagine you're a travel agent setting up a website that offers "Emotional Getaway" vacation packages. Write the description of your favorite spot for calming down. Include how you feel when you are there.

_____

_____

_____

_____

_____

_____

_____

_____

_____

... and more to do!

In the space below, draw yourself in your mental vacation spot. The next time you feel overwhelmed by a situation that makes you angry, imagine yourself being there.

17 releasing anger symbolically

for you to know

Holding anger inside is harmful for you but you can find ways to release your feelings symbolically.

Imagery and symbolism can help people cope with things that bother them in life. For example, parents in the Ojibwa Nation would hang dream catchers above their children's beds. The dream catcher was thought to trap bad dreams in the web that formed its center; good dreams would be allowed to flow down its feathers to the sleeping child. Then, in the morning, the sunlight would destroy the bad dreams that were caught in the web.

Another example of symbolic imagery is the "Wish-Giving Tree" in Shenzhen, China. Legend has it that in 1410, Tianhou, goddess of the sea, miraculously rescued the explorer Admiral Zheng. Tianhou later appeared to Zheng in a dream and instructed him to build a temple in her honor. A tree that was planted in the temple's courtyard still stands today, and people write down their problems on red slips of paper, which they attach to the tree.

This tree or a dream catcher don't literally take away problems, but they do release them symbolically, which is a wonderful way to cope.

Here are other symbolic ways to help you manage your anger:

- Write a letter to someone you are angry at. Tell that person what you really think and then tear up the letter.

- Imagine that a pillow is a person you are mad at and hit the pillow.

- Skip pebbles across a pond, letting an angry thought go with each one.

- Shoot baskets or kick a soccer ball toward a goal, imagining an angry situation with each shot.

- Write down your angry thoughts on a sheet of paper and then paint over them.

for you to do

This activity will help you symbolically release angry feelings you have been holding in. You'll need a balloon, small strips of paper, and something to write with.

On each strip of paper, write down something that made you really angry and that you haven't let go of. Next, roll each strip tightly and place it inside the balloon. Then blow air into the balloon, and as you do, focus on all the things you wrote down. After you have blown the balloon full of anger, hold the top of it closed. Take some deep breaths, say good-bye to everything the balloon is holding inside, and let it go. Watch as your worries sail across the room and are forever released.

... and more to do!

How did you feel physically after releasing your anger?

_____

_____

How did you feel emotionally?

_____

_____

Are there other feelings that you'd like to release (for example, sadness over a breakup with a girlfriend or boyfriend, stress over a family problem, or fear of failure in school)? Write them here.

_____

_____

Have you ever tried any of the symbolic releases mentioned earlier in this activity? If so, what did you do, and how did you feel after doing it?

_____

_____

_____

_____

18 relaxation techniques

for you to know

When you get angry, your body reacts. Your heart may race; your breathing may speed up; your muscles may tense. These reactions make it hard for you to think clearly and get control of your anger, so knowing how to relax is important.

Managing anger becomes easier when you are relaxed. You can use these helpful techniques when you want to calm yourself.

- Find a quiet location and get into a comfortable position. Starting at your toes and working all the way up to your head, tense your entire body, including your arms and hands. Hold that tension for a minute. Take a deep breath and let it out as you slowly release the tension from your head all the way to your toes so that you end up feeling like a rag doll. Repeat two or three times.

- Go to a spot where you won't be distracted or interrupted. Close your eyes and start to take slow, deep breaths, filling your lungs completely full of air and releasing it. Repeat several times until you feel yourself beginning to relax. Deep breathing increases the flow of oxygen to your brain, which helps you focus.

- Take a warm bath or shower and imagine washing away all of your anger. The water will help to relax your muscles.

- Read a book. Reading is a wonderful way to escape the world for a while. When you come back to reality, you'll be able to think more clearly.

- Take a nap. When you sleep, your body totally relaxes and goes into a meditative state. You'll wake up feeling more refreshed and ready to handle whatever is troubling you.

for you to do

We all have different ideas about what is relaxing. One person might think of a beach, a park, a cell phone, and an ice skating rink; another might picture a fishing rod, a book, a pair of running shoes, and an iPod. Using old magazines or newspapers, find images that represent your idea of relaxation. On a separate piece of paper, make a collage of these images. Put your collage in your room as a reminder of ways to relax when you're angry.

... and more to do!

Write down three activities that are your favorite ways to relax.

1. _____

2. _____

3. _____

Write down three new relaxation activities you would like to try.

1. _____

2. _____

3. _____

Which activity do you think will be most effective in helping you calm down?

_____

After you have tried one or more of your relaxation activities a few times, tell how they worked.

_____

_____

_____

handling anger 19
constructively

for you to know
Most of us can remember times when we regretted how we handled situations that made us angry. Instead of finding yourself in that position over and over, you can prepare yourself by thinking in advance about how you might react.

John had really done it this time. He was engrossed in his video game and had almost made it to a level he'd never reached before. Suddenly Cody, his five-year-old brother, charged into the room, flying his toy Stealth Bomber, and tripped, pulling the power cable from the wall. That did it! John picked up his video remote and hurled it at Cody, breaking a vase in the process. Cody started to cry. As John heard his mother coming toward them, he thought, "It was all Cody's fault, that little brat. Now I'm really in for it."

His mom came in and checked that Cody was okay. Then she looked around and noticed the vase. She asked John what had happened. When he explained, she said "John, no more video games today, and you'll have to clean up this mess. I know you were angry that Cody ruined your game. But you might have hurt your brother, and you broke my favorite vase. What else could you have done instead of throwing the remote at Cody?"

John thought about it for a while. Then he said, "I guess I could have closed my door. Or I could have told Cody how angry I was instead of throwing something at him."

for you to do

Read each scenario and respond to the questions.

Janet really needed to pull up her biology grade. As she was taking notes in biology class, Kyle kept throwing little pieces of paper at her. "What a pain," she thought. "If he does it once more, that's it!" As their teacher went on to describe the process of photosynthesis, Kyle pelted Janet with another piece of paper. Janet turned around in her chair, got in Kyle's face, and started to yell. She was escorted from class to the principal's office.

What are some of the consequences that Janet may face?

_____

_____

_____

What are some of the dangers in Janet's actions?

_____

_____

_____

How could Janet have handled the situation more appropriately?

_____

_____

_____

Tim had gotten his license six months earlier and he already had two traffic violations. As he started to change lanes, another driver pulled right in front of him and Tim almost rear-ended the car. "I've got to get by this dude!" he thought. He hit the accelerator, pulled around, and built up to 60 mph—in a 45 mph zone! Before Tim could slow down, police lights were flashing behind him.

What are some of the consequences that Tim may face?

_____

_____

_____

What are some of the dangers in Tim's actions?

_____

_____

_____

How could Tim have handled the situation more appropriately?

_____

_____

_____

... and more to do!

Tell about a time when you were angry and reacted poorly.

_____

_____

_____

_____

_____

_____

What were some of the consequences you faced?

_____

_____

_____

What were some of the dangers of your actions?

_____

_____

_____

What did you learn from this situation?

_____

_____

_____

Knowing what you know now, how could you have handled the situation differently?

_____

_____

_____

20 anger contract

for you to know

When you're caught up in anger, it's hard to tell people how to help you, so it's a good idea to have a plan to put in place before it happens. Letting others know that you are working on your anger and what they can do to help is a big step toward change.

Signing a contract is a way of making a commitment. It is like promising yourself that you will work hard to change your behavior. Sharing this commitment with other people—friends, family members, teachers, or other important adults—will help you honor it.

The first step is to decide what cues you will use to let these people know when you are getting angry. Your contract will also identify places where you can go to cool down and let others know what to do—and what not to do—when you get angry.

for you to do

Anger Contract

I am working on controlling my anger. As part of this change, I am making a commitment that you can help me with.

When I feel myself getting angry, I will give you one of these cues:

1. _____ 2._____ 3._____

If you notice that I am getting ready to lose my temper, please let me know by using one of these signals:

1. _____ 2._____ 3._____

I will then go to one of these places to cool down.

1. _____ 2._____ 3._____

Please do not do the following things. They only frustrate me more.

1. _____

2. _____

3. _____

When I have had a chance to cool down, I will return in a calmer frame of mind.

Signed by _____ Date _____

... and more to do!

Once you have drawn up your contract, think about whom you will ask to help you. Some possibilities include your parents, teachers, counselor, coach, siblings, and close friends. Write their names here.

Make several copies of your contract. Keep one for yourself and give the others to those you have chosen. Check off each name when you give that person a copy of your contract.

taking responsibility for your own actions 21

for you to know

When something goes wrong, it's much easier to blame others than to admit that we played a role in causing the problem. But blaming others doesn't resolve conflict; it just makes it worse. Before laying the blame on others, ask yourself, "What role do I have in this?" Once you learn to take responsibility for your own actions, you'll be less likely to push your anger onto someone else.

Tavaris knew that it was against the rules to have his cell phone at school, but he just couldn't resist sporting his new high-tech phone. He was sitting in Social Studies class when Joe asked to see his phone. Tavaris reached into his pocket and passed it back. As Joe was playing around with the phone, their teacher walked up. He took the phone and told Tavaris that his parents would have to come to school to pick it up. He also gave Tavaris detention for having a cell phone in class. Tavaris was ticked at Joe. It was all Joe's fault!

Ever been in a situation similar to this? It's clear that it wasn't all Joe's fault that Tavaris lost his phone or had to stay after school, but when you're angry it's easy to blame someone else for what happened. Tavaris needs to step back and look at the big picture. He can begin by asking: "How did I get myself into this?"

Nicole hated babysitting her little sister, Katie. Katie was constantly getting into everything. Nicole never could get anything done with her around. On this particular day, Nicole was supposed to be watching Katie while their parents were out. While Nicole was on the phone with her boyfriend, Katie got hold of their mother's red lipstick and played Picasso all over the living-room walls. When their parents got home, they were very angry with Nicole. She was placed on restriction for a month. Nicole thought, "This isn't fair! It isn't right that I'm the one getting in trouble. I didn't do it!"

Life ever treated you unfairly? In Nicole's case, rather than blaming someone else for the problem, she feels as though she's the one being blamed.

for you to do

Help Tavaris and Nicole step back and look at their contributions to the situations.

What role did Tavaris play in causing the problem?

_____

_____

_____

How could he have taken responsibility for his own actions?

_____

_____

_____

What role did Nicole play in causing the problem?

_____

_____

_____

How could she have taken responsibility for her own actions?

_____

_____

_____

... and more to do!

Briefly describe a time when you blamed another person for something you did.

_____

_____

_____

Have you ever been accused of something that you didn't do? What happened?

_____

_____

_____

Why do you think it's easier to blame others for your problems than to accept responsibility?

_____

_____

_____

The next time you find yourself either blaming or being blamed, what can you do to keep from getting angry?

_____

_____

_____

22 keeping perspective

for you to know

We all overreact to situations at times, but when it happens frequently it can lead to big problems. Keeping perspective means recognizing when you're blowing things out of proportion. You can then change your response so that the situation doesn't get out of control.

Katherine was having one of the worst days of her life. She had totally forgotten that her term paper was due, not to mention that she had overslept and was late to school. "Is this day ever going to end?" she thought. On her way to her next class, she noticed her friends Leslie and Jasmine standing next to her locker, looking mischievous. "What's up, guys?" she asked. "Nothing," they responded innocently and smiled at each other.

When Katherine opened her locker, her books were missing. "I am so not in the mood for this!" she said. She hit the locker, threw her backpack across the hall, and slammed her locker shut. She made such a commotion that everyone was staring and teachers ran into the hallway to see what was going on.

Leslie looked at Katherine. "What's your deal? Here are your books. We were just playing with you." Both Leslie and Jasmine walked off, leaving Katherine humiliated as everyone watched.

Ever had a Katherine moment? Odds are you have. It usually happens when you're having a bad day and any little thing can push you over the edge. Here's the good news: you can keep situations in perspective and stop yourself from overreacting.

To avoid blowing things out of proportion, Katherine could have tried the following:

- **Known her feelings:** Katherine knew she was in a bad mood. She could either have avoided her mischievous friends and gone to her locker later or just walked away when she opened the empty locker.

- **Spoken her feelings:** Rather than making a spectacle of herself, Katherine could have simply told her friends, "Look, I'm having a really bad day, and I am so not in the mood for this. Can you just give me back my books?"

- **Joked it off:** Since her friends were playing around, Katherine could have played back by saying something like, "Okay, that's funny, and you got me. Now I really need my books, so I'm not late for another class." This approach might have resulted in getting her books back quicker without an audience watching.

for you to do

Briefly describe a time when you blew a situation out of proportion.

_____

_____

_____

What were you thinking?

_____

_____

_____

What was the outcome of the situation?

_____

_____

_____

What could you do differently the next time you're faced with a similar situation?

_____

_____

_____

... and more to do!

How can being aware of your thoughts and feelings keep you from overreacting?

_____

_____

_____

If you repeatedly overreact to situations, how do you think it will affect your relationships with others?

_____

_____

_____

What are some consequences you have faced because of overreacting? (For example, have you lost friends or been suspended from school?)

_____

_____

_____

23 getting the facts

for you to know

Assuming that you know what others are thinking and feeling is a slippery slope that can get you into deep trouble. Rather than responding to situations with anger, it is important to be sure you have the facts straight.

Kristen had a really bad crush on Cole, a new kid at school. When she told her friend Lisa how much she liked Cole, Lisa asked, "Do you want me to do a little matchmaking?" "No! Don't say a word!" Kristen said. Lisa agreed that she wouldn't.

Finally it was time for lunch, and Kristen was looking forward to seeing Cole. When she walked into the cafeteria, she saw Lisa talking to Cole. When Lisa and Cole spotted Kristen from across the cafeteria, they smiled and waved. Kristin shot Lisa a dirty look. "What?" Lisa mouthed. "You know what!" Kristen mouthed back. She stomped across the cafeteria and in front of everyone gave Lisa a piece of her mind.

In this example, Kristen reacted based on her belief that Lisa had told Cole her feelings, but she didn't actually have all the information. Have you ever assumed you knew what was going on in a situation when in reality you didn't have a clue?

When you catch yourself making assumptions, do this:

- Say, "Stop it!"
  Every time you catch yourself thinking you know what someone else is thinking, tell yourself to stop.

- Think positively.
  Think of how you may be misreading the situation. Try to see other sides of the story rather than focusing on what you "think" you know.

- Realize that not everyone thinks as you do.
  What you think may be quite different from reality. Seek out the facts before you react.

- Ask yourself, "Am I jumping to conclusions?"
  You may not have all the information you need to make a decision. Do you react to information you've received from others rather than the person you're in conflict with?

- Ask for the truth.
  Go directly to the person and ask what's going on. What's the worst thing that will happen?

for you to do

Rewrite Kristen's story using the suggestions given earlier.

_____

_____

_____

_____

_____

_____

_____

_____

_____

_____

_____

_____

... and more to do!

Have you ever made wrong assumptions about a situation? Tell what happened.

_____

_____

_____

What happened when you found out that you were wrong?

_____

_____

_____

What might have happened if you had gotten all the facts?

_____

_____

_____

24 stages of anger

for you to know
Anger builds in stages. By understanding the progression of your anger, you can learn to quickly identify when you are becoming agitated and head it off before it gets out of control.

Alex's story can show you how anger progresses.

1. Your anger button gets pushed.

> *Alex was getting ready for his big soccer game. He looked at the clock; it was 5:15. He was supposed to be at the field in fifteen minutes, and no one was home to drive him. "Where are my parents?" he thought. He tried calling, but no one answered. Every minute, Alex became more agitated.*

Can you guess what Alex's button pusher is? If you guessed "being late," you're right!

2. Your thinking gets distorted.

> *While Alex was anxiously waiting for his parents to arrive, he kept thinking, "By the time I get there, the game's going to be half over and all the guys will be ticked at me! I'll probably be kicked off the team."*

Anger tends to distort how people think about situations. Notice how Alex assumed the worst-case scenario and blew things out of proportion. Other common distortions include blaming others and misinterpreting events.

3. Your feelings take over and you react.

When his dad pulled into the driveway and honked for Alex at 5:40, Alex rushed out of the house. His face was red, and he slammed his hand against the car. He glared at his father and shouted, "I can't believe you did this! The coach is going to get on me, and it's all your fault!"

Notice how Alex's feelings have taken control of his behavior. He was worried that he might be kicked off the team; he was embarrassed about facing the team and coach; he was hurt that his parents hadn't even thought to call him. Most of all, he was angry that he was going to be late.

for you to do

Once Alex's button was pushed, his anger quickly progressed. In the space below, write a new ending for his story. How could he have thought differently? How else could he have reacted?

_____

_____

_____

_____

_____

_____

_____

_____

_____

_____

_____

_____

... and more to do!

Think of a time when you were angry. Describe each stage of your anger. Then go back and circle the key words that indicate you were in that stage.

Stage 1. Your anger button gets pushed. (What really set you off?)

_____

_____

_____

Stage 2. Your thinking gets distorted. (How might you have misinterpreted the situation, blamed others, or blown things out of proportion?)

_____

_____

_____

Stage 3. Your feelings take over and you react. (What other feeling went along with your anger?)

_____

_____

_____

What do you think would be the best outcome of learning to change your reaction to anger?

_____

_____

_____

25 perception

---

for you to know

Your perception of any situation—what you think is happening—affects how you react. There is usually more than one way to look at any situation, but when you're in the heat of anger, it can be hard to step back and see clearly.

Mallory and Casey were at the movies. Mallory saw their friend Sarah sitting nearby with Noah, the boy Casey really liked. The two were whispering, their heads close together. Mallory couldn't believe what she was seeing. Were Sarah and Noah an item? How could Sarah? Casey's birthday was just around the corner. What a birthday present this was going to be!

Casey also noticed Sarah and Noah whispering together. "What are those two up to?" she thought. "They seem to be planning something. I wonder if it has to do with my birthday."

Mallory and Casey both saw the same thing but came up with different conclusions. Has that ever happened to you?

for you to do

Do you see this glass as half-full or half-empty? Changing the way you look at a situation can change the way you react. On the left, write down negative thoughts you have had about situations. On the right, reframe your thoughts so that they are positive.

Negative Thoughts

My friend didn't call me.
She must be mad.

_____

_____

_____

_____

_____

Positive Thoughts

She's probably been busy.
I'll call her.

_____

_____

_____

_____

_____

... and more to do!

Look at the pictures below. See if you can find a friend to do these activities with you.

In the picture on the left, do you see a vase or the profiles of two people? On the right, do you see a young woman or an old woman? If you can you see both, notice which one you see first. Show these pictures to a friend. Do you both see them the same way? If not, does that make one of you wrong?

Just as with these images, in life there are two or more sides to every story. Frequently we accuse others of being wrong simply because they don't see things the way we do. Wouldn't it be great if we could see all sides before we react?

for you to know

Some decisions are easier than others. Some don't require much thought at all, while others cause a lot of stress. One thing is certain: Decisions made in anger are likely to be impulsive and usually don't have good outcomes. That's why it's important to weigh your options before you react.

You will make many decisions in life. Some will be small, such as what to wear for the dance or which movie to see. Some will be big: Do you get into the car with your best friend even though he's been drinking? Do you go out with that cute guy even though he's got a bad reputation?

When you are angry, it is much harder to exercise good judgment when you have a choice to make. By making it a habit to think before you act, you can learn to react thoughtfully rather than giving in to anger.

for you to do

Several of Jeremiah's friends told him that a kid named Cody wanted to fight him after school. Cody had been running his mouth about Jeremiah since day one, and Jeremiah was sick of it. He wanted to finish this once and for all but wasn't sure he wanted to fight. So before he made a choice, he listed the costs and benefits involved. His list included these things:

- I might be expelled from school.

- I may have to go to court.

- I could hurt Cody badly.

- My parents will ground me for life.

- Cody could hurt me.

- I could get charged with assault.

- It will feel good to shut Cody up once and for all.

- Cody will learn not to mess with me.

- Others will leave me alone.

Help Jeremiah weigh his options—to fight or not—by deciding whether each item above is a cost or a benefit. Then write them in the correct column.

Costs of Fighting	Benefits of Fighting

Tell what decision you think Jeremiah made, and why.

_____

_____

... and more to do!

Think of a decision you have to make. Record what the decision is and weigh the costs and the benefits.

Decision to Be Made	
Decision:	
Costs	Benefits

Each time you have a decision to make, weigh your options by listing the costs and benefits. Looking at a decision that way often helps the answer become clear.

for you to know

Learning to change your thoughts about frustrating situations will help you control your anger. Some counselors use a simple approach called the ABC model to teach people how to change their thoughts about a situation.

Here's how the ABC model works:

A = Activating event (the situation that makes you angry)

You were working on your term paper and took a brief break. While you were away from the computer, your brother went to check his MySpace page. The lights flickered, and when you got back to your computer, your last hour of work was gone.

B = Beliefs about the event

Beliefs can be rational and irrational. Rational beliefs are accurate interpretations of the event; for example, "I lost my work because of a power dip." Irrational beliefs involve distorted thoughts, which were explored in earlier activities. For example:

- *It was all his fault!* (blaming others rather than taking responsibility; see Activity 21.)

- *I'll probably fail—if I ever get to finish!* (blowing things out of proportion rather than keeping perspective; see Activity 22.)

- *He always messes around with my things.* (making assumptions rather than getting the facts; see Activity 23.)

C = Consequences

You throw a book at your brother. You yell at him, telling him that you hate him and wish he had never been born!

The next step is to look at your beliefs and decide whether they are rational or not. If they are not, you follow these three steps:

1. Dispute your beliefs.
   Think: *"Maybe it was an accident. It's not like he has any control over the power. I should have saved my work. Maybe he didn't know I was using the computer."*

2. Set goals to avoid similar situations in the future.
   Decide: *"I want to protect my work as best as I can. I want to be on good terms with my brother."*

3. Create a plan to support your goals.
   Plan: *"I'll set the computer up for automatic save. I'll tell others when I'm working on something important. I'll apologize for the way I reacted and try not to automatically blame my brother."*

for you to do

Now it's your turn to put the ABC model to work. Think of a recent situation that made you angry. Use the model to help you work through your thoughts and actions.

What was the activating event (the situation that made you angry)?

_____

_____

What were your irrational beliefs about the event?

_____

_____

What were the consequences of those beliefs?

_____

_____

How can you dispute your beliefs?

_____

_____

What goals can you set to avoid similar situations in the future?

_____

_____

Create a plan to support your goals.

_____

_____

... and more to do!

The next time you catch yourself getting angry about something, use the ABC model to help you work through the situation. The model will help you to look at things from another perspective and change your irrational beliefs. You can create a visual reminder to use this model by making an index card with the steps on it. Keep this card in a place that is easily accessible so you can get to it quickly. Soon you'll be able to put the steps in place without even needing to refer to the card.

for you to know

Some reactions make it easier to resolve a conflict, while others make it harder. Being aware of your own style can help you learn to respond in a positive way. And since people react to conflict in different ways, it is also helpful if you can recognize others' styles.

Here are some common ways people react to conflict.

The Competitor: It's your way or the highway. You're bound and determined to win, no matter the cost. You blame and accuse others of being wrong. You're always right. You're going to get the final word in, if it's the last thing you do!

The Doormat: You let others take advantage of you. Saying no has never been easy for you, so you become a doormat for others to walk on, which makes you angry. But you won't say or do anything because you don't want to make anyone mad at you.

The Bolter: In difficult situations, you bolt! You avoid conflict at all costs, no matter how angry a situation has made you. You tell yourself that there's nothing you can do about it. You rarely find a solution for your problems. You just bottle them up. Needless to say, you have a lot of unfinished business.

The Team Builder: When you have a conflict with someone, you stay focused on what happened rather than launching an attack on the other person. You try to resolve the conflict by meeting in the middle, or compromising. If you can't compromise, you agree to disagree and move on.

Can you guess which approach is the most effective? If you guessed the Team Builder, you're right! Team builders try to understand a situation before reacting. By using good listening and communication skills, they are more likely to get others to listen to how they feel, making it easier to resolve a conflict.

for you to do

Read these examples, and decide which approach to conflict is being used. Write your answer in the space provided. Answers are listed at the bottom of the page.

1. Math had always been Jan's hardest subject. She constantly struggled in class and didn't understand her homework. Now her dad was on her case again about her math grades. "There is no excuse for your doing so poorly, Jan. I am sick and tired of getting calls from your math teacher. What do you have to say for yourself?" he yelled. She wanted to tell him how much trouble math was for her, but she was afraid that he would just get angrier! "Nothing, Dad. I'll try harder. May I be excused? I have some homework that I need to do," she replied. With that, Jan made a quick dash for her room. As soon as she was inside, she shut the door and leaned against it. "Oh, he makes me so angry!" she thought. _____

2. Matt's best friend, Jacob, really hurt him this time. Matt had told Jacob for months how he really liked Emily. How could Jacob have asked her out on a date? Matt felt angry but he was worried that if he said something to Jacob, he might lose his best friend. Maybe it wasn't worth saying anything. Emily and Jacob would probably make a better couple anyway. _____

3. Carrie caught her mom reading her diary. How could she? Carrie took a deep breath and said, "Mom, why are you reading my diary? I feel like you don't trust me, and that hurts my feelings." Together, Carrie and her mom talked about privacy and trust. By the end of the conversation, Carrie's mom agreed to respect her space. In return, Carrie agreed to share more about what was going on in her life with her mom. _____

4. Tara and Jamie were in a heated argument over their plans to go shopping. Jamie wanted to ask the new girl at school to join them, but Tara wanted to keep it to just the two of them. The bell rang to signal that lunch period was over, and as Tara got up to leave, she turned back to Jamie and said, "You're such a do-gooder!" That did it for Jamie. She got in Tara's face and screamed, "Maybe so, but you're a snob—a super snob!" Then she stormed off before Tara could say another word. _____

1. Bolter; 2. Doormat; 3. Team Builder; 4. Competitor

Next, choose the Bolter, the Competitor, or the Doormat example and rewrite it using the Team Builder style.

_____

_____

_____

_____

_____

_____

_____

_____

_____

_____

_____

... and more to do!

Think about how you usually react to conflict. Put a 1 next to the style you are most likely to use and continuing ranking the other styles from 2 to 4.

_____ The Competitor

_____ The Doormat

_____ The Bolter

_____ The Team Builder

If you use a different approach to conflict, describe it here.

_____

_____

_____

Ask several people who know you well how they think you most often react to conflict. Write down their responses here. Do most agree with the style you ranked first?

_____

_____

_____

Tell about a conflict you recently had. How could you have resolved it using the Team Builder style?

_____

_____

_____

_____

for you to know

I-messages express how you feel without making others feel that they are to blame. Learning to use I-messages instead of you-messages is a simple but important way to improve your communication skills.

You-messages focus on what other people have done in a way that makes them feel as though they are being attacked. These messages often include words that put people on the defensive, like "should," "always," "must," "ought to," and "never." When you start finger pointing and making accusations, people are likely to stop listening to you. Instead, they focus on what they are going to say in response to your attack.

An I-message tells what you feel, what the person has done to make you feel that way, and why you feel the way you do. By using I-messages instead of you-messages, you can decrease tension in a conflict. The other person is less apt to feel defensive, and it will be easier for the two of you to work out a solution to whatever situation has caused the anger.

Here are two examples:

1. You are angry with a friend who usually eats lunch with you but has been sitting at a different table all week.

   You-message: You always ignore me!

   I-message: I feel hurt when you don't sit with me at lunch because it makes me think that you don't want to be my friend.

2. You have been trying to tell your friend about a problem at home, but she keeps responding to each new text message she gets.

   You-message: You never listen to me!

   I-message: I feel angry when you keep texting while I'm trying to talk to you because it makes me think that you don't care about what I am saying.

Which message would you be more willing to listen to?

for you to do

Now it's your turn to try these messages. For each situation, write down how you would respond using a you-message. Next, change that response to a more helpful I-message.

The boy sitting behind you in class is using his pencil as a drumstick.

You-message: You _____.

I-message: I feel _____ when you _____ because _____.

Your friend totally humiliates you in front of the class by telling everyone who you have a crush on.

You-message: You _____.

I-message: I feel _____ when you _____ because _____.

Your group is supposed to present their project in class today. You find out that you are the only one who did any of the work.

You-message: You _____.

I-message: I feel _____ when you _____ because _____.

Your mother comes home from work. You've been cleaning the house but haven't gotten to your room yet. She accuses you of not doing anything.

You-message: You _____.

I-message: I feel _____ when you _____ because _____.

Another kid trips you as you are walking down the hall.

You-message: You _____.

I-message: I feel _____ when you _____ because _____.

... and more to do!

For one week, keep a tally of all of the times that you use you-messages. Notice whether they include the words "should," "always," "must," "ought to," or "never." On the table below, make a check mark for each time that you use a you-message that day. Next, in columns 3 through 7, place a check mark for each defensive word that you use in your you-message.

	You-Messages	Should	Always	Must	Ought To	Never
Monday						
Tuesday						
Wednesday						
Thursday						
Friday						
Saturday						
Sunday						
Total						

Add up the accusatory messages. Which of the statements did you use most frequently?

_____

Now that you are aware of using this language, how do you plan to change it?

_____

_____

_____

30 good listening

for you to know

By using I-messages to express your own feelings and building good listening skills that help you understand how others are feeling, you can defuse anger-provoking situations.

Communication is an important part of working through anger, and being a good listener is an important part of communication. Listening well helps you connect to the person you are upset with so that you can understand each other better.

Good listeners share these characteristics:

- They pay attention to the person who is speaking.

- They keep eye contact.

- They show interest by nodding or by smiling at appropriate times.

- They make sure that they understand what has been said by repeating it in their own words. For example, a good listener might say, "Do you mean that …?"

- They let the other person finish his or her thoughts without interrupting.

- They ask questions if anything is not clear when the speaker has finished.

for you to do

Think of a time when you were a good listener.

What was the other person talking about?

_____

What did you do to show that person you were listening?

_____

How did that person react?

_____

Now think of a time when someone listened well to you.

What were you talking about?

_____

How could you tell that the other person was listening carefully?

_____

How did being listened to make you feel?

_____

How can listening help defuse anger?

_____

_____

_____

... and more to do!

How often do you really listen to others? One great place to practice your listening skills is with a close friend. The next time you're with a friend, ask him or her a question. Then sit back and just listen.

Did you listen well?   ☐ Yes   ☐ No

If yes, which of the suggestions listed earlier did you follow?

_____

_____

If no, what did you do that showed you were not listening well?

_____

_____

What will you do differently in the future?

_____

_____

complimenting others 31

for you to know

Being complimented makes most people feel good on the inside. On the other hand, being torn down is likely to make someone feel horrible and often leads to angry feelings.

Amanda was in a very playful mood in gym class. She started to sing. Jenna, who was having a really bad day, quickly had enough of Amanda's singing and called out, "Girl, you can't sing! Have you ever heard yourself? Whoever said you could was deaf! Just shut up!"

How do you think Amanda felt after that verbal assault? She was probably embarrassed, hurt, and maybe a little angry. It's easy to use words to tear people down. But have you ever tried using words to build them up? You'll get a completely different reaction. Don't you feel good when someone pays you a compliment, like, "You look nice today" or "Hey, those are cool shoes"? You can do the same for others!

for you to do

Put a check next to each sentence you can use to compliment someone. Put an X next to those sentences that would tear someone down.

- ☐ Your help was really important.

- ☐ I am very proud of you.

- ☐ That's stupid.

- ☐ You never do anything right.

- ☐ You did a great job!

- ☐ You aced the test.

- ☐ You screw up all the time.

- ☐ You are really nice.

- ☐ I couldn't have done this without you.

- ☐ You're so lazy.

- ☐ I can't stand listening to you.

- ☐ You're hopeless.

- ☐ You're a great friend.

- ☐ You always listen.

- ☐ What a whiner you are!

- ☐ I can't tell you anything.

- ☐ You're so trustworthy.

- ☐ You're a nerd.

... and more to do!

Think of positive things people have told you that made you feel good. Write their statements in the speech balloons below.

32 body language

for you to know

Words are not the only way people communicate with each other. In fact, studies have shown that most communication takes place without any words at all!

The idea that you can communicate without speaking might seem strange, but it's true. Most communication between people takes place without words; it is based on body language. Your body language, also called nonverbal communication, is made up of your gestures, facial expressions, posture, and even your tone of voice. This language lets others know what you are feeling.

Look at some of the ways people use body language to express their negative feelings:

- rolling their eyes
- plugging their ears
- crossing their arms
- glaring
- sighing

- clenching their fists
- biting their lips
- gritting their teeth
- tapping their feet impatiently
- pointing a finger at someone

Not all body language communicates negative feelings. Here are some examples of positive messages:

- waving hello
- smiling
- hugging
- blowing a kiss

- patting someone on the back
- clapping
- giving someone a thumbs-up
- nodding in agreement

for you to do

For an entire day, notice how people communicate without words. Write down the body language you observe, the situation it occurs in, and what message you think it sends.

Body Language	What's Happening	Message

... and more to do!

Body language can sometimes be misread. For example, you might think that a boy who is making faces and rolling his eyes at you is making fun of you. But what if his contact lens is giving him trouble? Or you might think that a girl who is rubbing her hands together is cold, or perhaps worried, but it's possible that she just put on hand lotion. So if you're in doubt about the message someone is sending you, you might want to ask what the person means.

Have you ever misunderstood another person's body language? Tell what happened.

_____

_____

_____

Has anybody else ever misunderstood your body language? Tell what happened.

_____

_____

_____

_____

_____

_____

_____

---

for you to know

Anger is often a result of miscommunication or misinterpretation. Being sure that you have all the facts before you react, trying to see another's perspective, and discussing your feelings with that person are all important steps in controlling your anger.

Miscommunication occurs when people don't relay their ideas effectively. Here's an example.

Jose told Robert that he was going to the football game Friday night and that his parents could take Robert home after the game. Robert made arrangements with his own parents to drop him off at the game. He told them that he didn't need a ride home because Jose's parents were going to give him a lift.

Friday at the pep rally, Jose called across the bleachers that he couldn't go to the game. Robert didn't really hear him, but waved back. That night Robert went to the game and afterward looked everywhere for Jose. He texted him and left phone messages, but there was no response. Robert finally gave up and called his parents (who were out for the evening) to come and get him.

When Jose called on Saturday, Robert burst out, "Where were you, man? I had to get my parents to come for me, and they were ticked! They had made plans because I told them you'd give me a ride home." Jose answered, "I told you at the pep rally that I couldn't go. You waved back, so I thought everything was cool."

This is a classic case of miscommunication that might not have happened if Jose and Robert had spoken face-to-face.

Misinterpretation occurs when we don't have all the information and try to fill in the gaps—and get it all wrong. Look at the following example of how misinterpretation can have a negative outcome.

Alexa just couldn't wait to tell Victoria the exciting news: she had just been chosen to represent their school in a statewide competition. When she got to math class, she rushed over to the seat next to Victoria. When Joey came in, he found Alexa in his seat. "She's always trying to get under my skin," he thought. "She knows that's my seat!" He said loudly, "Get out of my seat!"

"In a minute," Alexa answered. "No, now. Move it before I move you," Joey retorted. "Chill out, I said in a minute," Alexa said, and she went back to whispering to Victoria. Meanwhile, Joey was getting angrier. He leaned forward and shoved Alexa—and ended up in the principal's office.

Have you ever misinterpreted a situation only to end up in trouble? Misinterpretation can be a web that traps you. Be careful not to make assumptions about another's behavior. If you get it all wrong, then you're setting yourself up for problems.

for you to do

Tell about a time when you were caught in a web of miscommunication or misinterpretation.

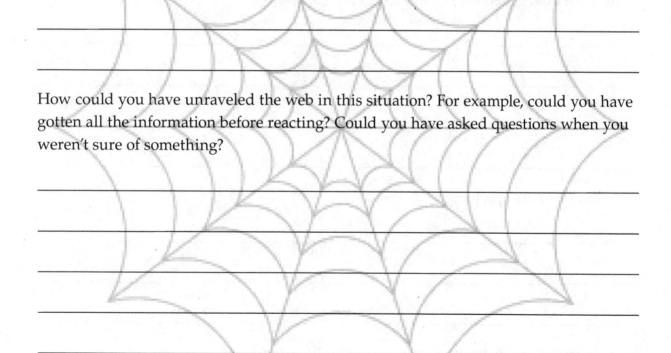

How could you have unraveled the web in this situation? For example, could you have gotten all the information before reacting? Could you have asked questions when you weren't sure of something?

… and more to do

Here's a fun activity to help illustrate how miscommunication occurs. You'll need a group of friends to play this game with you (the more people the better). Ask the last person on your list to report back to you so that you can record the final message. You can use text messaging, phones, e-mails, blogs, or any other type of communication. Just make sure your friends know it's a game!

Write down a statement that you're going to pass along.

_____

_____

Record the final statement that made its way back to you.

_____

_____

_____

_____

How did the message change?

_____

_____

_____

How do you think this activity applies to real-life situations?

_____

_____

_____

for you to know

Assertiveness means standing up for yourself and communicating your feelings without harming others or violating their rights. Being assertive, rather than passive or aggressive, is the best way to get along with other people.

In communicating, some people are passive and some are aggressive, but the ones who are usually liked best are assertive. Let's say you hear that a group of your friends are going to the movies on Friday night. You haven't been invited but would like to go. These three reactions can help you see the difference in communication styles:

Passive: "I'm not doing anything Friday night. Anything going on?"

Aggressive: "I'll be there. What time and where?"

Assertive: "I'd really like to join you. Is that okay?"

Being assertive means

- speaking up for your rights while still respecting the rights of others;

- calmly and clearly expressing how you feel;

- being confident;

- not letting others impose their feelings and beliefs on you;

- being able to say no.

for you to do

Read the following situation. Underline Jeremy's inappropriate or aggressive words and actions. Then rewrite the situation so that Jeremy is assertive. Some possibilities include asking to speak to his teacher after class, talking to her before his feelings had become so intense, involving a school counselor, or asking his parents to meet with his teacher. Can you think of others?

Jeremy hated math class. It seemed like no matter what he did, Mrs. Stewart was on his case 24/7. One morning, he raised his hand to answer a question. When Mrs. Stewart looked around the room and called on someone else, Jeremy rolled his eyes and let out a loud sigh. Later, when he leaned over to talk to a girl in the next row, Mrs. Stewart said, "Jeremy, I'm tired of your interrupting my class. You'll be staying after school for detention." Jeremy slammed his hand on the desk and burst out, "That's so unfair! No matter what I do, you're always on my case."

_____

_____

_____

_____

_____

_____

_____

_____

... and more to do!

These questions will help you see how assertive you are.

Do you volunteer your ideas even if they are different from others' ideas? ☐ Yes ☐ No

Do you ask questions when you don't understand something? ☐ Yes ☐ No

Do you say no without feeling guilty when you don't want to do something? ☐ Yes ☐ No

Do you speak up when others try to take advantage of you? ☐ Yes ☐ No

Do you face difficult situations rather than avoiding them? ☐ Yes ☐ No

Can you take criticism without getting angry? ☐ Yes ☐ No

Are you able to express your feelings and be receptive to how others feel? ☐ Yes ☐ No

If you answered no to at least three of these questions, you might want to revisit these earlier activities:

Activity 29   Using I-Messages

Activity 30   Good Listening

Activity 32   Body Language

Activity 33   Communicating Clearly

Remember, you have the right to express how you feel about things. You have the right to say no. You have the right to speak the truth. You have the right to disagree. You have the right to be you! The more you practice being assertive, the easier it will become.

35 steps toward change

---

for you to know

It's likely that throughout your life you will face the need to change. Changing yourself is not easy; it takes time, energy, and motivation. But you can do it!

Your response to anger can change if you

- recognize your anger is a problem;

- explore ways to change your response to anger;

- practice the skills you've learned.

How long does it take to change your response to anger? Some experts say that to move from being a very angry person to a moderately angry person takes about ten weeks. So be patient with yourself. It is also important to remember that you may find yourself going back to your old ways of handling anger at times. If that happens, revisit your anger goals and reaffirm your commitment to reaching them.

for you to do

Go back to Activity 3 and review the anger goals you set for yourself. Write down those goals and the action plans you came up with, and record your progress.

Long-Term Goal:

_____

_____

Action Plan:

    1. _____

    2. _____

    3. _____

What steps have you taken to meet your long-term goal?

_____

_____

_____

If you have not yet reached this goal, what more can you do to help you get there?

_____

_____

_____

Short-Term Goal:

_____

_____

Action Plan:

1. _____

2. _____

3. _____

What steps have you taken to meet your short-term goal?

_____

_____

_____

If you have not yet reached this goal, what more can you do to help you get there?

_____

_____

_____

... and more to do!

When I feel myself getting angry, I can

1. _____.

2. _____.

3. _____.

4. _____.

5. _____.

These people can help me manage my anger:

1. _____.

2. _____.

3. _____.

4. _____.

5. _____.

I will try my hardest never to

_____.

The most important thing I have learned about managing my anger is

_____

_____.

The answers you have just written down are like a snapshot of what you have learned and how you have changed. Congratulate yourself!

36 seeing how far you have come

for you to know

When you first started this workbook, you were having a hard time handling your anger. By completing these activities, you have probably learned a number of ways to manage your angry feelings.

At this point, it is likely that you have seen a change in your behavior and that others have noticed as well. What you have learned from doing the activities will not prevent you from ever experiencing anger again, but you will know how to keep it under control. See how far you have come!

126

for you to do

For each of these statements, circle the answer that best describes you.

I have improved my response to anger.

1	2	3	4	5
strongly disagree	disagree	neutral	agree	strongly agree

I have more control of my anger.

1	2	3	4	5
strongly disagree	disagree	neutral	agree	strongly agree

On average, I get really angry …

1	2	3	4	5
every day	every few days	once a week	every two weeks	once a month

Read each statement and check either "Yes" or "No."

People have noticed a difference in how I handle situations.	☐ Yes	☐ No
I have learned different ways to cope when I feel frustrated.	☐ Yes	☐ No
I have involved others in helping me when I get angry.	☐ Yes	☐ No
I know I can change how I handle situations that make me angry.	☐ Yes	☐ No
I have not hit anyone since I have been working on my anger.	☐ Yes	☐ No

The higher you rated yourself on the scales, and the more frequently you checked "Yes," the less anger is a problem for you.

... and more to do!

Look back at Activity 1 and compare your answers.

What areas have you improved in?

_____

_____

_____

What areas do you think you need more work in?

_____

_____

_____

Congratulations. You did it! You have accomplished a lot by completing the activities in this workbook. You've learned

- to understand your anger and how it affects you;

- what things push your anger buttons;

- how your family may play a role in your response to anger;

- how your body responds to anger;

- that anger can be a positive force;

- how to chill out and defuse your anger;

- to change the way you think about situations;

- good communication skills;

- that you can change.

To celebrate all that you've accomplished, photocopy the certificate on the next page and fill it out. Post it in a spot where you will see it often!

Certificate of Completion

This certificate is proudly presented to

_____

Your Name

for completing the activities in

The Anger Workbook for Teens

Dated this _____ day of _____, _____

Congratulations on all of your hard work!

For every minute you are angry,
you lose sixty seconds of happiness.

—Ralph Waldo Emerson

Raychelle Cassada Lohmann, MS, LPC, has worked in middle school and high school settings as a professional school counselor. She has done extensive research in anger management and specializes in individual and group counseling for anger management.

Foreword writer **Julia V. Taylor, MA**, is author of *Salvaging Sisterhood*, *G.I.R.L.S.(Girls in Real Life Situations)*, and *Perfectly You*. Taylor has worked as a middle and high school counselor and speaks nationally about relational aggression, body image, and other teen issues.

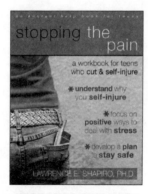